Revealing
The Skin

Revealing
The Skin I'm In

The Naked Truth About
'Nip and Tuck' Plastic Surgery

DR SANJAY PARASHAR

PARTRIDGE
A Penguin Company

Partridge books may be ordered through booksellers or by contacting:

Partridge India
Penguin Books India Pvt.Ltd
11, Community Centre, Panchsheel Park, New Delhi 110017
India
www.partridgepublishing.com
Phone: 000.800.10062.62

Dedication and Acknowledgements

My gratitude to these people knows no bounds:

My father Shri Yadunath and my late mother Smt. Malti who brought me in to this world, guided me into becoming the man that I'm today. They gave up a comfortable life in the village to see all their five children educated. Through my father's sheer determination and hard work as a trader, taxi driver and vendor, he provided for all of us and made everyone in the family successful in life. My mother gave her all-out support to these dreams, giving up her own comfort and personal ambitions. And I owe so much to my siblings who to this day remain supportive of one another: Tarun, Vinay, late Arun and Sadhana.

Sangeeta, my wife, my daughter Sanjana and my son Sidhant: I'm forever grateful for your continued support, patience and encouragement. You all inspire me to continue to be the best husband and father I could ever be.

My mentors, who taught me unselfishly and shared their expertise in terms of my practice and speciality. Their time invested in me will never be forgotten and will be passed to those who will need it, to keep their legacy in me, intact.

My most sincrere gratitude to Dr Sonone who identified my skills and, being an ambidextrous himself, taught me to train both my hands. Dr Pankaj Maheshwari, Dr Uday Bhat, Dr Mukund Jagannathan, Dr Ashok Gupta, Dr Tariq Saeed, Professor I T Jackson, Professor David David, Mr Tony Moore and many more.

To my colleagues who remain loyal, your support in what I do is deeply appreciated.

And above all, to my patients and my clients, you who have edified, trusted and helped me all these years, you could never imagine how thankful I am to you for making me grow, professionally and personally.

I'm who I am because you are who you are.

Disclaimer

This book is written as a guide for people who are interested in the subject of plastic surgery. The author and its publishers have taken every care in preparing and writing the book, but they accept no liability for any errors, omissions, misuse or misunderstandings on the part of any person who uses it.

The author and publisher accept no responsibility for any damage, injury or loss occasioned to any person as a result of relying on any material included, omitted or implied in the book.

The personalities and incidents featured, humorous or otherwise, are not meant to disrespect any institution or any person. All patients' rights to confidentiality has been protected by the author and shall remain as such.

Note:

All the proceeds from this book
will be used to finance surgery for children
who require it.

Contents

Welcome

My name is Sanjay Parashar and I am a plastic surgeon.

Plastic surgery is an intensely personal subject which causes a great deal of debate, often very emotional debate at that. Perhaps more than any other branch of medicine, it is also surrounded by a dense, almost impenetrable fog of rumour, myths and misconceptions.

I am writing this book because I want to blow that fog away.

I have no particular interest in using this as a vehicle for selling my services. I don't need to; I'm doing fine the way things are, thanks.

But I want you to be fully briefed with clear, accurate data on the subject, so you can think about it, discuss it and—should you need to—make the right, informed choices about it.

Here's what we're going to be talking about:

- **The history of plastic surgery:** people think of it as a modern day science but it's actually been around for nearly 3,000 years.

- **What plastic surgery can—and can't—do for you:** all the things you should think about and evaluate if you're contemplating a course of it for yourself. In this section I also describe exactly what happens in the surgeon/ patient consultation process.

- **Potential perils and pitfalls:** we're going to take a close look at malpractice, insurance and things that can go wrong. I am not going to flinch about this or gloss over any unpalatable considerations; these are all things that you need to know.

- **How to choose the right surgeon:** I'll tell you all the questions you need to ask and even give you some coaching on how to ask them.

- **The cost of plastic surgery:** why do some practitioners charge so much less than others?

- **My responsibilities as a plastic surgeon:** ethics, etiquette and confidentiality. I'll also talk about your responsibilities as a patient—and yes, you do have some, as do the families and friends of patients.

- **The things I've learnt over the years**: about denial, taboos and the danger of plastic surgery addiction.

- We're also going to look at **plastic surgery as a career:** whether or not you're thinking of pursuing it yourself, I hope this will give you a useful added insight into the profession.

- We'll take a look at **corporate social responsibility**, what it means to my profession and I'll tell you more about where the proceeds from the sale of this book will go.

- Finally, I will present you with a selection of **testimonials** from my own files.

I hope you'll spare the time to join me on this educational journey, because I honestly think you'll find it fascinating.

Let's get started . . . .

The History of Plastic Surgery

As I mentioned at the outset, plastic surgery is thought of as a modern day phenomenon, but its origins can be traced back as far as 800 BC. Its undisputed progenitor is Sushruta, a surgeon who practised near a place that we now call Varanasi, on the banks of the Ganges in India.

His collected textbooks, Sushruta Samhita, describe over 300 surgical procedures and 120 surgical instruments. They were used as a point of reference for many centuries.

Another key player is Charaka, who lived slightly later than Sushruta. He is considered to be one of the first exponents of Ayurvedic medicine and is credited with discovering and explaining the concepts of digestion, metabolism and immunity.

For these breakthroughs, along with many other pioneering works and his philosophy that prevention is better than cure—which may seem obvious to us now, but was revolutionary at the time—he is known as the father of Indian medicine.

The work of these two giants eventually made its way westward when they were translated from Sanskrit into Arabic in around 750 AD. From there, the practice spread further and started to be adopted in Europe. In Italy, the Branca family of Sicily and a Signore Gaspare Tagliacozzi of Bologna familiarised themselves with the surgical techniques described by Sushruta and started using them to great effect.

For many generations, India remained the epicentre of the practice. Word of the amazing work that was being done there began to spread. In the late 1700's, several British physicians started travelling there to observe the rhinoplasties—nose and facial surgeries—that were being performed by native methods.

A report on one succesful rhinoplasty, performed by Kumhar Vaidhya, appeared in an English magazine in 1794. Of course in those days, no academic qualifications were required to practice medicine; although Mr. Vaidhya was evidently an excellent surgeon, he was actually a potter by trade!

Another British surgeon, Joseph Carpenter Caprue, spent 20 years in India studying local plastic surgery methods. On his return, he used his learnings to perform the first major surgery in the Western world in 1815, using the very same tools and instruments that were described in Sushruta's books, with only minor modifications.

But ironically, and as in so many other fields, the greatest and fastest advances in plastic surgery were brought about by war, especially the devastating World War I of 1914-18.

This "war to end all wars" killed millions and caused countless horrific injuries. The medical profession had never before had to find a remedy for so many terrible facial and head traumas. In the past, shattered jaws, blown off noses and gaping skull wounds meant—simply, starkly and certainly—death. The advent of plastic surgery brought solutions that were literally life saving; solutions that could even allow patients to resume a normal life.

These hugely beneficial results, sometimes hailed as miraculous, catapulted the science into a new realm of public awareness and acclaim. Thanks to massive new influxes of financial investment, some of the best medical talents in Britain, France, Germany, India, Russia and Austria-Hungary were able to devote themselves fully to creating innovations and improving techniques.

As World War I continued on its deadly course, the press made great play of showing shattered faces that had been rebuilt by the new surgery procedures, with the aim of restoring hope among the deeply demoralised populace.

It was an easy and logical step for the surgeons to realise that those same techniques could also be used for disfigurements caused by factors other than war, and even to enhance beauty.

Suddenly, a ray of hope was shining for the many people who had spent their lives in deep, shameful embarrassment because of a physical peculiarity.

And the rest, as they say, is history.

The aesthetic surgery industry was born and it boomed. As well as facial surgery, additional procedures were developed to include body contouring techniques, such as breast augmentation, liposuction and "tummy tucks".

As the years have gone by, the demographic has changed. Once the exclusive preserve of the rich and famous, aesthetic surgery is now accessible to all and increasingly affordable.

People are simply flocking to have appearance enhancing procedures. In 2007, more than 11.5 million of these procedures were carried out; an astonishing increase of 50% on the figures from the year 2000.

What Plastic Surgery Can— and Can't—Do For You

Let's begin by clarifying the definitions, as there are several terms in use. Some of them mean much the same thing, some of them denote a marked difference—and there are a few grey areas in between.

The umbrella term is **plastic surgery**. Plastic comes from the Latin word plasticus, which means something that can be moulded. Nowadays, of course, if you say the word "plastic," most people immediately think of those substances, usually made from petrochemicals, which can be used to make more or less anything and everything.

So there's an unfortunate association that if something is "plastic," it means that it isn't quite "the real thing"—and that association sometimes rubs off on plastic surgery. My solution is to go back to the roots of the words and think of it simply as "surgery that moulds."

Then there's **cosmetic surgery**, which is defined as "the procedure that modifies or improves the appearance of a physical feature, irregularity, or defect." I don't much like this term; it implies camouflage, superficiality, the stuff you read about celebrities getting done to themselves.

Cosmetic surgery is perceived to be less serious, more "fluffy" and therefore less technically difficult than plastic or reconstructive surgery. It's associated with less risk, less pain and shorter recuperation. Most patients also think that cosmetic surgeons require significantly less training than plastic or reconstructive surgeons. Not true; they may well—and quite often do—*receive* less training, but that shouldn't mean they *require* less training.

There are countless horror stories about unqualified people performing disastrous procedures on unwitting patients (and, by the way, we will be talking about this in full later.) All too often, these unqualified people tend to refer to themselves as cosmetic surgeons. I think by now you can probably guess what I think of the term!

Next is **reconstructive surgery**, whose meaning is self-evident. As much of my work is primarily reconstructive, I would be quite happy to be called a non-cosmetic plastic surgeon—although that doesn't mean that there isn't a beautifying element in what I do.

Finally there's **aesthetic surgery**, which has similar goals as reconstructive and cosmetic surgery, so it bridges and unites the two disciplines. Aesthetic surgery is fundamentally scientific, but it also involves an artistic approach during the surgery, to achieve a harmonious result.

Aesthetic surgery is performed to maintain or restore appearance, correcting things like a crooked nose, bat ears, saggy breasts, a sagging face, baldness, or a protruding tummy. Via procedures such as breast enlargement, lip enlargement and buttock enlargement, it can also be used to enhance appearance.

OK, so what can it do?

Well, first and foremost, it can make you feel better about yourself and more comfortable with who you are. A recent study conducted by David B. Sarwer PhD, an Associate Professor at the University of Pennsylvania School of Medicine, found that a year after receiving aesthetic surgery, 87 percent of patients reported satisfaction with it, including improvements in their overall body image and the body feature altered.

They also experienced less negative body image emotions in social situations.

But you're probably wanting to know, will it make you more attractive?

As the saying goes, beauty is in the eye of the beholder. It would be a dull world indeed if every one of us had exactly the same reactions when we looked at someone else and decided whether we found them attractive or not. And of course there's that other saying that beauty is more than skin deep; there are literally thousands of other factors that add to—or subtract from—a person's attractiveness.

But let's get real.

It's a plain fact that everywhere in the world, regardless of social and ethnic differences, people broadly agree on what the conventional norms of human physical attractiveness are.

And to a greater or lesser extent, we all do what we can to enhance and accentuate our own attractiveness: we tidy our hair, we brush our teeth, we "spruce ourselves up," we wear clean clothes, we choose styles and colours that we think suit us, and so on.

It's also a proven fact that people who comply with those norms of attractiveness, who are generally considered good looking, get preferential treatment. They tend to do better in life. They tend to be more confident, sociable, well adjusted and capable. Sorry, but that is true. Please don't shoot the messenger!

And the fact is, aesthetic surgery really can help people to achieve or at least get much closer to that preferential state. I have thousands of case histories which prove this point.

At one end of the spectrum, I treated a two year old child who was born with some of his fingers and toes fused together and some parts of his fingers missing. Within three months of surgery, he started using pencils and toys and his creativity blossomed.

I also remember a 28 year old man who felt obliged to hide himself away and wear a veil, to hide the large unsightly tumors growing out of his face and ears. It only took one session of surgery to remove the deformities, but that one session enabled him to get a job and live a normal, socially interactive life.

And here's one of the most amazing cases I've dealt with: the client was morbidly obese, weighing around 250kg. For five years she had been confined to living in one room, as she couldn't get out of it. She had a gigantic stomach and needed help just to manoeuvre it on and off the bed.

I worked alongside a highly qualified nutritionist who designed her meals and controlled her intake to the last morsel. A physical therapist helped her to build her cardio vascular and physical stamina; she was going to need it because ultimately I was going to perform an operation to remove the protruding stomach.

There was no doubt, this was a high risk operation with the potential for numerous complications, even including a fatal outcome. But eventually she was deemed fit enough to undergo the procedure. The protruding part of the tummy was removed; it weighed an astonishing 20kg.

There were some worrying post-operative moments. But after about ten 12 days, the patient was up and about. When I saw her two years later, she was 115 kg—still a fairly large size but less than a quarter of what she weighed before! She was fully mobile, enjoying her life to the fullest and still working hard to reduce a little more.

At quite the other end of the spectrum, a young, beautiful girl asked me to create a dimple for her. After I had done it she told me, "I love to smile nowadays and I look for every opportunity to do it." There's no doubt it was a non-essential procedure. But was it wrong? You can decide for yourself; that girl and I already have.

I'm happy to admit that I too have benefited from aesthetic surgery. I had a premature hair loss condition which made me feel insecure and older then I was. After an excellent course of hair transplantation I could feel my confidence growing. I became much more socially active and the change was so much more than just skin deep. I used to have stage fright, but now I relish any opportunity to be in the spotlight.

Would have this have been possible without the transplant? Yes, maybe.

Could that sort of personal change be brought about through other methods, such as hypnosis or life coaching? Yes, maybe.

Did plastic surgery do the trick? Yes, 100 per cent undoubtedly.

As recently as the 1970's, mental health professionals generally held the opinion that if people sought plastic surgery, they had psychological issues that required treatment. This has now been disproved by numerous studies. The desire to have plastic surgery is not necessarily a pathological compulsion; it could just as easily be a simple choice.

So what happens when you go to see an aesthetic surgeon?

The human anatomy is designed with an infinite number of variables, so that every person's physique and features are unique, distinctly created by a Supreme Being. As surgeons, we endeavour to make sure that, for every patient, we add value and enhancement to their natural attributes.

The first step in this process is the consultation. The patient comes and says whatever they want to say, in as much detail and depth as they can, describing their perceived problem and how it affects them in their personal and physical life.

The second stage consists of a full evaluation to identify any related illnesses, allergies or previous surgeries that could affect the outcome of the envisaged procedure.

An aesthetic assessment comes next. This involves careful inspection of the relevant parts of the face or body, fully documented for future reference. Important decisions will be based upon this assessment, so it has to be done in great detail.

All the steps that I've just described can quite often be done in one session. But in some cases I may feel the need to do further assessments to formulate a definite solution and strategy. I may ask for more photographs, I may want to go away, do a bit of research and spend some quality time in thinking about the case. I make no apology for taking time over this; a hasty, snap decision is not what is called for here.

Once I have defined a way forward, I ask the patient to come back for another consultation. I go through all the options, describe the procedures and supply all the relevant considerations that the patient should be aware of. I may make a recommendation, but the final decision must be made jointly by the patient and I.

After this, I insist on a cooling-off period, giving time for both of us to revise or even reverse the decision we made. This is vital for both parties. As they say, haste makes waste.

With the cooling-off period completed and the decision firmly formulated and agreed on, my team proceeds to provide all the written information and resources the patient might need. These reading materials help the patients to acquire more knowledge about pre and post operation, with especial emphasis on aftercare, once the patient goes home. the team then draws up a schedule and books the appointment for the procedures and all the follow-ups required.

I ought to add that I always reserve the right to decline a request for surgery. I will normally make this decision very early on in the process, so as not to waste anyone's time or cause unnecessary disappointment. But if something comes to light farther down the line, which was previously unknown or undeclared, and which has a bearing on my decision to perform the procedure or not, I will never adopt the attitude of "too late to stop now."

Honesty and truth are always the most important virtues for us. Whenever I see a patient, I say what's on my mind and I offer a solution only if I would happily apply the same solution to my loved ones.

What can't it do?

But let's go back to that mention of pathological compulsion which I mentioned earlier, because I don't want to gloss over this or dismiss it. Let's go into it a little more deeply . . . .

People turn up at my clinic for all sorts of reasons and with all sorts of motivations.

External motivations come from outside the mind and body. They can be positive or negative and they're usually about avoiding pain rather than actually gaining anything. For instance, the trigger could be about escaping from ethnic prejudice or age discrimination. Or quite often, the person might have just been coerced into coming to see me by a spouse, peer group or parents.

Internal motivation is the desire to diminish depression, shame and social anxiety, by altering the features the person dislikes about themselves. People with this kind of motivation usually express a desire for a more youthful appearance or career enhancement.

For me as the surgeon, the crux of it is understanding what the patient really wants. Sure, they may say that the surgery to give them a new nose, or whatever, will make all the difference. But they may still feel just as wretched after the bandages come off. The difference is that their bank account will be a little lighter too and this could make them feel even worse.

So I ask questions. Lots of them.

I try to look at everything through the eyes of the patient and ask "will this solve the problem or is there something else?' I set out to discover if there is a 'secondary gain' involved beneath the initial actions and thoughts.

It's like peeling away the layers of an onion to reveal the truth. Once I fully understand their way of thinking and agree that their stated objectives have a good chance of being realised through a surgical procedure, then we can move forward.

And if I don't think my skills can solve their problem? Under those circumstances, I simply won't operate.

Not least because the person in question will never value the job I've done and will always consider themselves to be ugly.

A bit more about body Image and imagined ugliness

On many occasions a patient describes a problem which is significantly or even totally invisible to me. In fact there can appear to be no physical deformity present at all. In this case they are probably victims of dysmorphic body disease or 'imagined ugliness'.

This is a mental condition in which relatively normal appearing people completely misperceive their appearance; they develop a subjective feeling of ugliness related to a tiny physical defect which is far less noticeable to anyone except themselves.

Sadly, it's extremely common.

Hours spent in front of a mirror wondering "what's wrong with me" only feeds the mis-imagination and can actually create a negative hallucination.

What happens next is awfully predictable. This issue blows up out of all proportion and the 'ugly spot' becomes the reason for a lack of career success, failed relationships, low confidence and self-esteem. It can cause real distress, anxiety, depression, and neurotic tendencies.

It's a fear and not an actual deformity, but to the patient it is 100% real.

In those cases, I will most likely suggest that they weigh up their options with someone who deals with the emotional side of their problem first.

I don't want to bang my own drum too much, but it's unfortunately true that if I refuse to do the work they have requested, they will just look for someone who will do it; and there are far too many of these unscrupulous practitioners around.

But that's their choice.

In summary:

Through aesthetic surgery, I can help you improve and enhance your appearance—often quite dramatically—which can directly lead to you being more confident, more at ease, happier and more successful.

But no amount or type of aesthetic surgery can, in itself, solve deep seated issues you may have about your own personality and self-worth.

Naturally, I take every case individually. So until and unless we meet for a consultation, I have no way of knowing if I think aesthetic surgery would help you or not.

But I can promise you I will be totally honest.

Perils and Pitfalls

This is going to be a long and exhaustive (although I hope not exhausting) chapter. By the time you get to the end of it, you may think that I'm actually trying to persuade you NOT to have aesthetic surgery.

That's not the case, of course. But I do want you—or anyone else—to have the best possible experience and outcome, both short and long term. One way to make sure you have that is to make sure you know what can possibly go wrong.

Let's start with something that can go wrong right at the start of the process, or even before . . . .

The dangers of self diagnosis

We live in a world where information about anyone or anything is available anywhere, at the touch of a button. Your smartphone, laptop or tablet allows you to search for any subject and get whatever you want, in seconds or even sooner.

For instance, I just Googled the word SURGERY and was presented with 491 million results in 0.42 seconds. Astonishing (and isn't it even more astonishing that we take it so much for granted nowadays?)

But beware: the fact that one set of information shows up higher on the search engine rankings than other websites, videos or articles, only makes it more likely that you'll read it; it doesn't make it more likely that it's accurate. Following up on that search for SURGERY, one of the top three results describes itself as "the official master guide to all types of surgery." Official? According to which authority? Master guide? Who says?

As well as straightforward, honest information and insights, you also get sales pitches (some better disguised than others), opinions, horror stories and expressions of bias. What is true, what is rubbish and what someone has merely posted because they've had a bad day, all comes jumbled together.

This wouldn't be a problem except when people use the internet because they have some sort of medical concern and they attempt to diagnose it for themselves. It's true to say that the exact answer they need will be available somewhere, but It's also perfectly likely that they won't find it.

The problem gets worse when someone stumbles over something that is simply wrong, but it lodges in their mind and becomes a kind of truth.

I've seen that happen too many times. So many patients have come to see me with their own biased, self concocted diagnoses that they got online. The tragedy is, there are some doctors who can be coerced into giving the patient the treatment they have read about and decided that they need, or who are too happy to just do it and take the payment.

I think it's a major contributing factor in surgeries that have gone wrong. Yes, that is only my opinion, but it's based on years of experience and observation of the industry I know and love.

So please, surf with caution.

Let's be careful out there

As I promised at the outset, I'm not going to flinch from any unpleasant aspects of my profession.

Wherever there is a business demand for a product or service, market forces come into play; and those forces can be more focused on profit to the supplier than benefit to the receiver. So perhaps the recent explosion in cosmetic surgery was inevitable. It's driven by demand from consumers, but it's just as much driven by the prospect of big financial rewards—and perhaps a degree of glamour—for the suppliers.

You see, the most appalling thing is that insufficiently trained people can set up in business and start advertising their wares after learning just a handful of procedures. There are a worrying amount of established "institutes" and "societies" who train and churn out underqualified, inexperienced "cosmetic surgeons" who can go straight into the market.

So the harsh end-truth is that not everyone involved is a qualified plastic surgeon. There are many who have just jumped on the bandwagon, with catastrophic consequences.

Try another Google search: enter PLASTIC SURGERY HORROR, add the country where you are and see the awful tales unfold.

Here are a few from just the last couple of years, taken only from Dubai, the city where I practice:

- In 2008, police raided a flat where untrained 'surgeons' were carrying out cut-price cosmetic surgery. None of them were qualified, the surgical implements were lying alongside kitchen utensils on the draining board in the kitchen and the staff were re-using surgical gloves.

- In 2010, a French doctor was performing a breast enlargement on a 24-year-old Belarusian woman. He gave her the wrong injection, which killed her. He was formally charged with practicing without a license.

- In the same year a British surgeon was jailed for leaving unskilled medical personnel in charge of a patient who was undergoing liposuction. Without proper medical attention, this simple procedure was botched and this patient died too.

I believe that the term "plastic surgeon" or any of the associated terms should be reserved and licensed specifically to those who trained for it; in fact it's absolutely scandalous that it isn't.

I don't say this from a selfish or elitist standpoint, merely to reduce that unending torrent of horror stories and damaged lives. Although 'repair' work is actually very lucrative for my practice, I would much prefer people to get it right first time, not least for the psychological damage it can cause, which even I can't repair.

How to pick a good surgeon and how to avoid a bad one

There's another complication: the fact that patients will travel across the globe to find the right surgeon makes it an international business. And that fact in itself makes it devilishly difficult to regulate. There are lots of legal loopholes that can be exploited—and I'm afraid that's exactly what happens.

A spot check survey in 2003, carried out in London by the National Care Standard Commission, investigated 22 clinics. Its main and most worrying findings were that many private clinics failed to carry out basic checks on the identity of their surgeons, and many of them advertised benefits which could not possibly be true, like "amazing looking skin in under an hour".

Staying in the UK, as recently as 2010, the senior teaching hospitals cooperated on an even more comprehensive survey: the National Confidential Enquiry into Patient Outcome and Death, which revealed a disturbing picture of an industry that is far too relaxed about putting patient safety at risk.

The report highlighted the ongoing absence of strict controls, despite a succession of whistle-blowing investigations like the one in 2003. It was especially significant that one in 10 of the clinics approached had ceased to exist before the study was completed, suggesting a rapidly shifting and unstable industry.

I believe there is a need for a completely transparent, universal code of practice, which specifies the information that must be provided to patients before they consent to undergoing surgery. As well as protecting the patients, it would also save reputable surgeons from being tarred with the same brush as unscrupulous practitioners.

I can't honestly see when or even if this change will come. But if you are a choosing an aesthetic surgeon, you should be suspicious of any establishment that is not happy to give full, detailed replies to your questions about its credentials.

We are certainly happy to do that and more at my practice. We rigorously practice self-regulation, we comply with all municipal rules and both we and our partners are completely certified to carry out what we offer. I see it as a moral obligation.

Let me say this yet again because it's vital: whatever you do, don't assume that just because someone is set up in practice, they have already been checked and approved. There's every chance that they haven't. They may not even be sufficiently qualified.

Here's a checklist of the things you should ask about—and you should be fully satisfied with the answers—before you go anywhere near agreeing to a procedure:

- Who exactly is the surgeon who will perform the procedure?

- Does he or she have a relevant qualification and experience? Although they may have a degree of expertise, it may be for a different part of the body. For instance, an ear, nose and throat specialist might carry out a breast enlargement, because that's what a client has demanded, not because they are legally licensed or trained to do it.

- Do they offer a large menu of procedures, from breast enlargement or reduction to liposuction and nose straightening? I'll talk a bit more about specialization later but a menu that is too extensive can be a danger sign. It implies a mindset that is thinking "if you're willing to pay for it, we're willing to do it."

- How many of this type of procedure do they perform in a year? If it's less than 20, it probably isn't enough to amass quality experience.

- Are they confident that the operating theatres are properly equipped? Would they be willing to have it inspected?

- Will an anaesthesiologist and resuscitation team be on hand during the procedure?

- Do they offer a cooling-off period, so that after an initial discussion the patient can go away and decide whether to have the operation?

- Are they fully insured for any eventuality?

- Do they offer psychological counselling?

- Do they actively seek patient feedback?

- What is the follow-up to the procedure, if any?

- Do they have systems in place to monitor the quality of clinical practice?

- Do they offer financial incentives and discounts in their advertising? If they do, avoid them like the plague, no matter how attractive the offer is. Remember, there is no such thing as cheap surgery and properly qualified surgeons simply won't offer it.

Until we get that worldwide legislation and code of practice that I talked about, I'm afraid the only person who can be relied on to carry out a full audit of the surgeon's credentials is you.

I know this is an awfully long list of questions and you may be daunted about asking them all. But many aesthetic surgery procedures are either impossible or extremely difficult to reverse, and I think you should bear that in mind before you decide not to bother getting all the facts checked.

And please remember that you can be persistent and methodical about asking questions without being unpleasant or aggressive. A reputable surgeon will be only too happy to see you being so thorough. So just keep calm and keep asking!

It's all about attitude

I live and work in Dubai, which is the heart of the Middle East and more or less at the centre of the Western and Eastern worlds, in terms of both geography and culture. Without wanting to generalise too much, I have noticed a big difference in the perception of plastic surgery within those two cultures.

In the Eastern mindset, plastic surgeons are almost considered to be magicians who can do no wrong and whose pronouncements should never be questioned.

In the West, because of the amount of press that is given to celebrities getting plastic surgery, it is often more associated with vanity and its practitioners are seen as a lower caste to other doctors; suppliers rather than an experts. I have heard them described by a Westerner as "tit and bum surgeons who charge a lot." True in some cases, but not by any means all!

And neither of these attitudes are helpful when you need to make an important, informed choice.

When I've talked to many patients from India and Pakistan, I've found that they just don't want to hear about complications. They don't believe in them. They only want to know the good and positive things. The moment I mention issues for and against the operation, they tend to get apprehensive and they don't even want to consider the possibility that they could actually have complications themselves.

It's undeniably flattering to have so much faith placed in your abilities and I often hear patients say "you're the expert, you do whatever you want." And of course, a positive outlook is enormously helpful when it comes to healing. But full and open two-way dialogue is even more important.

Apart from anything, you need that dialogue with the surgeon so you'll know exactly what is happening when the procedures are in course. I remember once, after conducting a cleft palette repair on a child, the parents asked when we were going to operate! They didn't realise the job was done.

"Doctor when will you do Plastic Surgery" Becos they have weird imagination of Plastic surgery that can remove all defects without any scars.

On the other hand, Westerners can often have a list of requirements that are too demanding and unrealistic. I've had patients tell me the exact geometric angle that they want their nose to be. Sometimes they bring photos of celebrities and tell me they want that nose, or those lips or cheeks.

Naturally, we do all we can to achieve the result that the person desires, but let's remember we're talking about organic, human material here, not computer graphics. Let me talk you through the options and their various pros and cons, then we can jointly make a realistic, achievable decision that everyone is happy with.

That's a hallmark of a successful surgery.

One more word about attitude

This is just an illustration of different global attitudes. In some parts of the world, people don't like to admit that they've had an aesthetic procedure and, if you suspect that they have, it's seen as rather impolite to ask them straight out. In others, if people have had such a procedure, they're disappointed if nobody notices or comments on it, so they can give them all the details; it's a huge status symbol.

During a visit to Iran, I saw lot of women going about their daily business with splints on their noses. I commented to a local colleague that the aesthetic surgery business must be thriving here. He replied that many of these women haven't actually had surgery; they just want to look like they could afford it if they wanted to!

OK. Let's push on with those perils and pitfalls.

What about insurance?

Insurance companies have a different stance on plastic surgery compared to any other medical specialty. I suppose this is a by-product of the lack of regulation that I've been talking about in this chapter. So it may be understandable that anything that comes from the plastic surgeon's office is looked at suspiciously by insurers. But it's also extremely frustrating, both for me and some of my patients.

Imagine a cancer on the face. It can easily be removed by a general surgeon or an oncologist whose aim is purely to rid the cancer from the body, which is fair enough, but they may pay little or no attention to the appearance afterwards. With their effective combination of qualifications, skills and objectives, plastic surgeons can get rid of the cancer too, but also make sure the patient looks presentable to society afterwards.

It's the same with a stomach hernia, which is a bulge you can see or feel. The bulge is made up of fat and bowel that has slipped through a weak spot in the muscles in the abdomen. It can be repaired relatively simply by a general surgeon, but it usually leaves a big scar. I've seen some awful hernia scars that look as if they were made with a tin opener.

A plastic surgeon would find a less visible access area, go through that, make the repair meticulously, then cover the wound to leave little or no deformity.

Plastic surgeons also have—and this is exclusive—new technology and innovations that can shrink chronic skin wounds within weeks, making them so small that they may not even be visible afterwards. The more traditional alternative is months of healing and very noticeable after-effects that can remain visible for life.

So a qualified plastic surgeon can actually be a more desirable option, but the insurance companies rarely see it that way; they continue to regard us as a high risk category.

There have been some instances which buck this trend. But in general, if you're considering plastic surgery and you're hoping your medical insurance will pay for it, by all means ask—but don't get your hopes up.

Personally, the only times I've ever seen insurance companies soften their attitude to our industry was when one of them wanted treatment for their own people or a family member. Then the money was found.

Generalist or specialist?

I could be accused of contradicting myself here; I'll leave that for you to decide.

In my checklist of questions you should ask a potential surgeon, I advised you to be wary of clinics or practitioners who provide too long a menu of procedures they're willing and able to perform for you. I still stand by that, as it implies that they're more interested in your money than in you.

However, there's been a recent trend for people who specialise in just one procedure and nothing else, such as breast enlargements; rather like those auto services who only change your exhaust or tyres. And I'm not sure it's a trend I like.

In my opinion, a modern plastic surgeon should be an all rounder, able to deal with any part of the body, able to combine aesthetic sense with medical skills, totally conversant with all procedures and equipment.

A surgeon who ticks all these boxes will always be a better choice because of the understanding they have of the end result—how the individual procedure will harmonise with the rest of the body—and the vast extra knowledge they bring to the operating table.

There are also very important practical and cost considerations if you want more than one procedure—an eyelift, a facelift and some liposuction for instance. A good generalist surgeon can easily do all those himself for you, quite possibly in one session, greatly reducing the cost of the surgery and the time you, the patient, has to devote to it.

So I would advise you to ignore the buzz about specialisations.

Avoiding complications

It goes without saying that life is full of risk. And it would be folly to deny that your life is more at risk when you are undergoing a medical procedure than when you are, say, sitting on a sofa watching TV.

Things can go wrong. Complications can ensue. It happens.

But it is possible to reduce the possibility of complications by treating each step of the procedure with military precision and taking every possible precaution.

At my practice, from the first contact with a new client to the post operation checkups, we pride ourselves on making sure neither side experiences any unwanted surprises.

We settle for nothing less than a thorough evaluation of the physical, psychological health of the patient, a full evaluation of the area to be treated and a detailed surgical action plan.

Close follow-up is another key element. In most situations there are warning signs which a good surgeon will pick up and pre-emptively treat to prevent adverse developments.

But I believe that the most important factor is an open communication line between the patient and the clinic. We positively encourage any questions and work hard to remove the burden of worry from the patient. And we try to engage and involve them fully, paying especial attention to their part in the post operation management process.

We certainly do not go further or take the next step in any process until the client is satisfied with the answers.

So I really hope you're satisfied with what you've read so far. Let's move on.

The Price of Plastic

People often comment about the huge expense of plastic surgery. "Why do such short operations cost so much?" they ask.

It's a trend that seems to have increased recently. Maybe it's a result of the economic uncertainty of these times, which is making people more cost-conscious and likely to shop around; maybe it's because so many price quotes are available online. Whatever it is, at my practice we've never experienced so many phone calls and emails that ask no questions except the cost of all kinds of different procedures—treating fractured arms, removing gall bladders, performing breast enlargements or tummy tucks.

The problem is, as far as I'm concerned, there's no set answer.

If you call a car repair shop and asked them how much they charge to repair a dent, naturally they're going to say "it depends on the dent." Are we talking a scratch or a near write-off? A rather crude analogy perhaps! But I'm sure you can see where I'm going with this. The cost of a tummy tuck, for example, will depend on the tummy.

One patient may need two hours while another one might need four, depending on their existing condition. The follow-up and aftercare timings can also vary, depending on the amount of possible complications involved.

I guess there is a possibility of offering a 'pregnancy style' package; something like two visits, one operation and three checkups afterwards. But the business doesn't really work like that—at least it doesn't the way I run it.

To help you appreciate the true value of the practice of plastic surgery, I'd like to share with you some of the costs that are involved in a basic operation. I'm not going to deny that it does mount up, from the initial consultation up to post operation checkups, as many varied resources are used in order for us to arrive at the desired result.

And with no disrepect to the car repair industry, the people who work for me have to be quite a lot more qualified!

The manpower complement

Successful plastic surgery comes through people.

The team is a vital part of a practice's resources. They are like the gears that make the wheels of our practice turn.

It all starts with the receptionist. She has to be a well trained and friendly person and although she receives and manages the calls that go in and out of the clinic, she's much more than just the lady on the telephone. She establishes the open communication line between surgeon and patient and makes sure that the patient—who may understandably be feeling a little nervous and insecure—feels welcome and comfortable at all times.

A nurse assists the surgeon when they see the patient for consultation. She too has to contribute to the feelgood factor that we want around the patient at all times.

There's a patient coordinator who handles the affairs between the patient and the hospital for scheduling purposes and a clinical coordinator who makes sure that the patient is received and carries out all the logistic requirements.

A hospital nurse must always be on standby, to prepare the patient for the surgery.

A couple of ward boys transfer the patient from the ward to the operating room.

Two nurses work in the operating room and an anaesthesiologist is required to be present throughout as well.

A specialist post-operative nurse needs to be on hand after the surgery to assist and oversee the stabilisation process.

Each and every professional is paid a salary to do their respective jobs. And if you want to attract and keep good people, you have to be prepared to pay competitive rates. Fact.

Then there's the surgeon, the hiring of the facilities, plant and equipment, the operating room and the medicines used. Even the way the place looks is a factor; when a patient walks in, they want to feel that they are in a thoroughly professional, place that is dedicated to one sole purpose, not someone's converted apartment.

And that all costs money.

OK—you could look at this line-up and say it's excessive, that some of the tasks such as the patient coordinator and the clinical coordinator could be combined, that I could probably do with one or two less nurses, that I could cut a few dollars here and there.

I could, but the blunt answer is I don't want to. I want our practice to run on the same lines as the world's very best hospitals. Not just for the sake of prestige or bragging rights, but because it makes things as smooth as possible and makes the risk of complications as small as possible for the patient.

And that has to be the overriding factor, every time.

Free consultation you say?

You see quite a lot of clinics offering a free consultation. Having read this far, you probably won't be surprised to hear that I'm not in favour of them.

In my opinion, the concept of free consultation dilutes the true value of the process. Consultation is every bit as vital as the procedure itself, as it's the time when the plastic surgeon's opinion and recommendations are discussed with the patient. At this vital first meeting, all the details should be discussed thoroughly and the processes explained.

If you go to a clinic that is offering this segment free of charge, do you think they will really put themselves out to make sure the consultation is conducted professionally? Or will they be more likely to make sure that it's conducted quickly? A no-brainer, I think.

I've also encountered people who think that because it's just talking, it shouldn't have a cost attached. "Oh, I just want to come in and have a chat with you," they say. "How come you want to charge me for that?"

It reminds me of the famous story of the factory owner whose machinery had stopped working. He called in an expert, who walked around the building looking at all the different parts. Then he opened his tool kit, took out a small hammer, tapped a pipe once and the machinery sprang instantly back into action.

When the invoice came, it was for $500 and the manager flipped. "How can you charge so much when all you did was hit a pipe?" he demanded.

So the expert sent a revised invoice with a more in-depth breakdown of the service, which read:

- Tapping the pipe—$10

- Knowing where to tap it—$490

That's my funny answer. But seriously, we're not just meeting for a coffee and a chat. If you come into my office it's for a specific reason. I'll be discussing your problem with you and by the end of it, I will have a workable solution for your relief and full satisfaction.

I'll be legally bound to give you the best advice possible that I can, using my expertise and experience.

When I'm not working with clients, I'm also in a cycle of constant re-training to keep fully updated with new insights, new technology and best practices. I will happily go abroad to make new discoveries and learn new techniques which can help my practice and expand my competence to higher levels. Although I graduated years ago, I still buy educational books, CDs and videos to add to my medical resources.

I've spent thousands of dollars on this and, to be frank, I think it's perfectly reasonable to pass at least some of those costs on to the people who also benefit from them.

If you believe there are cheaper options other than talking to me, and I dare say there are, please feel free to take them. The internet can give you a number of answers, although some may be wrong and even harmful if taken out of context.

By the way, you're always perfectly free to take my advice then find a cheaper surgeon afterwards to actually carry out the procedure.

But I believe that if you the knowledge you want to gain is truly important, as this is, and you want to be assured that you get the entire truth, you're best advised to pay an expert for it.

That's why I will always charge for a consultation.

A matter of conscience

Once again, please don't think I'm only saying this to make the maximum amount of cash, because this is something that cuts both ways; there are lots of times when I've told people I don't want their money. Not a penny of it.

These are the occasions—and there have been many—when I've been faced with a highly emotional patient who tells me they've been saving money for their entire life for a surgical operation that "simply has to be done." Quite often at these moments, I can see at a glance that they'd be wasting their hard earned cash because the physical difference that it will make for them is minimal. And of course that's exactly what they don't want to hear.

Sure, I could do the operation and some people I know would say I should go ahead anyway; after all, it's their money and it's what they want. But what happens in the all too likely event that they're disappointed with the result?

They'll blame me, they'll blame themselves, they'll blame everyone involved in the process, including the people who said "do it" and the people who said "don't do it." They might never be able to settle back into their old life the way it was. It's not too far fetched to say they could end up a lot more prone to anxiety, stress and depression. They will undoubtedly badmouth plastic surgery—and me.

Each case is different and I must consider the entire situation each time, but I think I can safely say this: if a flat chested young girl comes to me wanting a breast enlargement, I am more than 90% likely to go ahead and do it. The procedure is straightforward and the positive difference is obvious. In the eyes of society she will look—and more importantly she will feel—more attractive. Even though she's spent time saving money for it, my overwhelming experience tells me she will feel that she really got her money's worth.

But if I see a patient who has in my opinion a perfect nose, but who feels it could be improved, even if he too has been thinking about it and saving all his life, I will almost definitely refuse to do the surgery. I know it would be difficult to satisfy this patient and he would end up looking at the result and feeling low. The changes would most likely prove not be cost effective. So I'd just say sorry, I don't think this is right for you.

Finally . . .

I did promise at the outset that I'd be honest. Even so, I appreciate that I might have come across as a bit uncompromising in this chapter. But it's your body and your health and I don't think that's something that should ever be compromised with. Agreed?

Confidentiality and Ethics

I have made it my life's work to try to improve people's lives by giving them the help they need. That professional purpose gets me out of bed as soon as I wake up and puts me to sleep with a smile. I wish everyone had a job as fulfilling as mine is to me.

But more and more, I find that I have to work to maintain that positive attitude. Maybe I'm dreaming of a past that never really existed, but I'm sure the world has turned so much more commercial and consumerist. And yes, I do yearn for simpler times, when a patient would come in with a problem, the doctor would sit and advise on it, present the options, help the patient to make the decision and then to follow the recommended course.

Nowadays the patient comes in with a predetermined list of things gleaned from a combination of the internet, modern trends and the latest, cleverest marketing. The surgeon agrees to do it and the patient then goes through with it, irrespective of whether it will work for them or will not and whether it'll be safe in the future. It's purely about the money.

I mention that here, because I believe it makes it more important than ever before to establish and uphold a set of defined professional obligations. Many of mine are self imposed and I must say, once again, that not everyone in the business of plastic surgery is as scrupulous about them.

Confidentiality

I respect the privacy of my patients. As a clinic we do not give, sell, rent, or loan any identifiable information regarding customers or website visitors to any third party. Patients can rest assured that every piece of information we gather from them is held with the utmost care and will not be used in ways for which they have not consented.

Each staff member is dedicated to upholding these standards in all communications and records. Staff, patients, family members and visitors all sign a confidentiality statement and agree to keep all knowledge or information of our staff, patients and family members away from any third parties. Whether it's a member of the Royal family (VIP), a celebrity or some guy who lives in your street, we go to the same lengths to protect the anonymity of everyone who enters our facility.

You'd be amazed at how often we get calls out of the blue from a friend, spouse or family member, wanting to know how So-and-so is doing.

Unless we are absolutely 101% positive and know for a fact that the caller is genuinely someone in the person's very closest circle, we refuse to divulge any details. Not a scrap. Even then, we don't go any farther than the most basic possible information. If there is something specific that we need to tell a spouse, partner or close family member, it has to be done face to face—no alternatives can be considered.

For a wide variety of reasons, people use all sorts of tricks to persuade me or my staff to reveal what we know. Some of them are very good too. They should give out Oscars for amazing performances from people who are determined to get to the bottom of a big story or precious secret. We could regularly supply some nominees!

It's a tricky one, because we do also appreciate the anxiety that a loved one can face when they feel left out of the loop; the work being done will no doubt have a substantial impact on their lives and maybe their finances too. But it's still not my role to breach client confidentiality.

This is one of the reasons why I advise patients and their loved ones to create a support network if possible and use it while the treatment is ongoing. It means that even while we are ethically constrained to withhold information at that time, they can talk to each other and burdens and concerns can be shared.

By the way, you will notice that in other parts of the book, I talk directly and in some detail about cases and patients. But needless to say, I never name names and I can guarantee that there is no way you will ever associate the person I discuss with someone you may know or meet.

Ethics

I won't try to re-invent the wheel here. This is a code of ethics that has been around for some while and is used by numerous

---

hospitals and medical institutions around the world. We use it at our practice too and it pretty much says it all.

Consider first the wellbeing of the patient. The physician should consider the wellbeing of other patients, of society and of colleagues, as well as his/her own wellbeing, but that of the patient being treated at the time must be the physician's primary concern.

Practice the profession of medicine in a manner that treats the patient with dignity and as a person worthy of respect. Respect for persons is a fundamental principle of medical ethics; it excludes not only exploitation and discrimination but also discourteous and insensitive behavior.

Provide appropriate care for your patient even when cure is no longer possible, including physical comfort and spiritual and psychosocial support. The physician should try to ensure that all the patient's needs will be met.

Consider the wellbeing of society in matters affecting health. Practice the art and science of medicine competently, with integrity and without impairment.

Contribute to the development of the medical profession, whether through clinical practice, research, teaching, administration or advocating on behalf of the profession or the public.

Engage in life-long learning to maintain and improve your professional knowledge, skills and attitudes.

Continuous learning is necessary to maintain one's competence. Attitudes are central to the patient-physician relationship.

Resist any influence or interference that could undermine your professional integrity.

Refuse to participate in or support practices that violate basic human rights.

Promote and maintain your own health and wellbeing.

And I think that's the key to success. As long as you follow a certain code of ethics, as long as you feel that what you do is honest and truthful, as long as you communicate clearly to the patient, more often than not, you will have a positive outcome.

For another great set of ethics, you can't do better than the famous Hippocratic Oath. Written by Hippocrates, the father of Western medicine (or possibly one of his students) in the 5th century BC, it's a historical tradition for all medical practitioners to swear to it when they first start to practice.

Nearly everyone has heard of it, but few are familiar with what it actually says. So it's worth including it here:

The Hippocratic Oath

"I swear by Apollo, the healer, Asclepius, Hygieia, and Panacea, and I take to witness all the gods, all the goddesses, to keep according to my ability and my judgment, the following Oath and agreement:

To consider dear to me, as my parents, him who taught me this art; to live in common with him and, if necessary, to share my goods with him; To look upon his children as my own brothers, to teach them this art, without charging a fee; and that by my teaching, I will impart a knowledge of this art to my own sons, and to my teacher's sons, and to disciples bound by an indenture and oath according to the medical laws, and no others.

I will prescribe regimens for the good of my patients according to my ability and my judgment and never do harm to anyone.

I will not give a lethal drug to anyone if I am asked, nor will I advise such a plan; and similarly I will not give a woman a pessary to cause an abortion.

But I will preserve the purity of my life and my arts.

I will not cut for stone, even for patients in whom the disease is manifest; I will leave this operation to be performed by practitioners, specialists in this art.

In every house where I come I will enter only for the good of my patients, keeping myself far from all intentional ill-doing and all seduction and especially from the pleasures of love with women or with men, be they free or slaves.

All that may come to my knowledge in the exercise of my profession or in daily commerce with men, which ought not to be spread abroad, I will keep secret and will never reveal.

If I keep this oath faithfully, may I enjoy my life and practice my art, respected by all men and in all times; but if I swerve from it or violate it, may the reverse be my lot."

Every word of this oath I follow to the letter, and it may or may not work for everybody, but to me, it has borne much fruit in abundance. Even after 26 years of practice, I'm still learning and experiencing what following this oath is all about!

Now It's Your Turn: The Responsibilities of the Patient

Yes, that's you. It's a cliché but it's so, so true that if we don't have health, we have nothing. And I believe we should take it as a personal responsibility to do what we can to maintain our health, especially in this day and age when there are so many stress-related factors that can adversely affect it.

If it happens—and it does happen to most of us now and then—that we have to consult a doctor, there are things there too that we need to be mindful of.

Live the healthiest life you can

Remember Charaka, the Indian surgeon we talked about in the very first chapter? He was the one who first coined the proverb that an ounce of prevention is most definitely more effective and efficient than the corresponding pound of cure. Making healthy food choices, getting plenty of exercise, resolving stress, getting enough sleep, moderating alcohol consumption and refraining from smoking are those good habits we are all familiar with—and most of us need to work on.

Be respectful to providers, doctors and staff

Just as it's a patient's right to expect respect, it is the patient's responsibility to show respect in return. It makes life go so much more smoothly and pleasantly.

Be honest with the doctor

As an empowered patient, you recognise that being totally honest with your practitioner is imperative. This means sharing all information about your habits and health. Holding anything back can mean not getting the care that you need.

Complying with the treatment plan

Since you and your doctor will have worked together to agree on a treatment plan, it only makes sense to follow it. Not doing so renders the exercise pointless. But remember, ultimately, the only one who will suffer the loss is you.

Prepare for eventualities

For anyone who has medical challenges and/or takes prescription drugs to maintain their health, it's important to be prepared for adverse situations. If you find yourself in an emergency room, you'll want to be sure the hospital personnel know about the treatments you are already receiving, or the cautions needed for effective treatment.

Don't believe everything you hear in the news

We see stories every day about some new study or technology that changes the way certain diseases or conditions are treated. Sometimes the headlines don't tell the whole story. As an empowered patient, you know to look behind those headlines.

Make responsible decisions

In the face of a frightening diagnosis or a scary treatment option, it's difficult to leave our emotions out of our decisions. But you really need to make sure your decisions about your care are based on solid evidence and proven procedures, rather than wishful thinking.

Understand prescription drugs and their possible effects

There are so many possibilities for drug-related medical errors that we need to take responsibility for checking and verifying the prescriptions we're handed, then comparing them to the medication the pharmacist delivers to us. This is a safety precaution we should all bear in mind.

To learn more about potential side effects of any drug you're taking, this About.com website is good:

http://drugsaz.about.com/

Meet your financial obligations

There's no question that medical costs can become difficult and cumbersome, but they do need to be dealt with responsibly.

Respect your doctor's time and make sure you keep your appointment

These days, it seems all of us are under time pressure, but it's more acute for doctors than most other people, because if they're delayed, it often means that other people are delayed as well. It can even be injurious to someone else's health. So please be on time.

Be realistic in your expectation

Everybody responds differently to treatment. Don't expect your progress or outcome to be the same as someone else who underwent the same treatment as you. A good doctor will always help you anticipate a realistic outcome; please take them at their word and don't expect an outcome that hasn't been proposed.

One last thing—open the door to dialogue

If you've had surgery and you look markedly different, make it easier on the people around you by opening the conversational door and let them know about it. I understand this can be difficult, but it really is worth the effort. The more you can talk about it with people close to you, the better you're likely to feel about it and the quicker you'll get used to the difference.

Family and Friends Have Responsibilities Too

Here are some do's and dont's for people around a patient who's just had surgery. If you yourself are the patient, it might be worth leaving this book open at this page, or tactfully asking the folks around you to read this section.

Think before you speak

If you see someone with facial bandages or clearly showing the after-effects of surgery, please don't blurt out "my God! What happened? Are you OK?" Yes, you're only expressing your natural concern, but it's probably the last thing they want to hear.

Especially just after surgery, they will undoubtedly be feeling ultra-sensitive about their appearance, so avoid any exaggerated reaction.

Even if you're dying to know, don't come right out and ask if they've had a "nose job or "eye job". Say something like "you look great, like you've just spent a month at a health spa."

That lets the person let you in on the details if they want to, without being put on the spot. (Remember this tactic also if

---

you suspect someone is pregnant. There is no exchange more embarrassing than when one person says, "when is the baby due?" and the other responds, "there is no baby, I'm just fat." Or even worse: "I had the baby three months ago.")

Don't criticise

If someone tells you they're considering aesthetic surgery, no matter what your own views are, please try not to adopt the automatic stance that it's a bad idea. Respect their ability and right to decide for themselves. On the other hand, please don't say something like "you certainly could do with it!"

If a person tells you they've just had some cosmetic surgery done, the tactful thing to ask is if they're pleased with it.

It's serious

Please bear in mind that although it may be "aesthetic," it's still surgery, which is always a serious and often a delicate subject. Please try to resist the temptation to gossip or joke about it.

Be solicitous

When people tell you they've had cosmetic surgery, the first thing to ask is how they're feeling, both physically and mentally. They will appreciate it.

The Things I've Learnt Over the Years

This is a miscellany, covering facts, experiences and opinions around the subject of plastic surgery—along with a few of my own very personal secrets.

What's good is what you don't see . . . .

If you're driving a car, you don't normally notice a good driver, because they don't do anything to draw your attention. You do notice the guy who cuts you up and turns with no indication.

If you're watching a sporting event, you don't normally notice a good referee, because they let the game go on without drawing attention to themselves. You do notice the one who keeps stopping the action and makes bad decisions.

Sometimes, the things that are good are the things you don't notice.

So it's an inescapable fact, but it's also rather a shame for my profession, that you don't normally notice when someone has had good plastic surgery—unless of course it's intended to attract attention, like a breast enlargement. Otherwise, the plastic surgery that you do notice is plastic surgery that's been badly done and looks unnatural.

. . . and what's bad gets too much press

Following on from that point, you don't get to read about the many thousands of plastic surgery procedures that go off without a hitch (except in this book!) But if you believe everything you read in the media, you would get the impression that botched cases are the norm and successes are a rare exception.

This word "botch" is an interesting one. The media love to use it, especially when they can put it in the same sentence as the name of a celebrity. But they didn't invent it; it's actually been around for centuries. I must admit, it's highly applicable to my profession, as its original dictionary meaning is "an inflamed sore on the body." But it's used nowadays to mean any kind of job that it marred by a mistake or a mess.

As well as being used inaccurately, in my opinion it's also used far too loosely.

For instance, many procedures involve making an incision, so there is always a possibility that the incision will not heal perfectly; there's also a strong possibility that the incision will attract a minor infection while it heals—it's a physiological fact of life—and that can result in a small amount of scarring.

As another example, once liposuction has been performed, there is a common possibility that there may be some lumpiness remaining around the affected area. A good surgeon will make sure the patient understands this possible complication before undergoing the procedure.

These are things to be avoided if possible, of course. But if they do occur, it is hugely unfair to say they are "botched jobs."

By all means, the media should report on wrongdoings, malpractice and mishaps; like it or not, their audience wants to hear bad news. More importantly, they should track down and expose those ill-qualified, money-oriented surgeons who really shouldn't be practising.

But all journalists are trained to only report what is true, to avoid presenting speculation and opinion as facts and never to exaggerate the truth for the sake of a good story. It's up to them whether they choose to observe or ignore that training later, but those are the pillars of good journalism.

So please, let's have a sense of proportion with this.

The credibility of the press

While I'm talking about the media, I'm not going to leave it unsaid that, on more than one occasion, I have been approached by journalists who have offered to write about me favourably if I give them free treatment.

To me, that is bribery, which I do not engage in or allow in my practice. It also says something to me about some of the people who work in that profession and how likely they are to abide by those pillars of responsible journalism which I just described.

Too much is what a patient expects

There's a saying among plastic surgeons: "if it looks all right, it's too tight. If it looks a little loose it's all right." In other words, for the sake of a good, natural looking result that will stay that way for longer, we avoid going too far in tightening the appearance.

Quite often, the patient wants to go farther than the surgeon recommends, but there's another saying: "the enemy of good is better."

It all depends on how you look at it

One day a woman came into my office. She had two very large moles, one on one cheek and an even bigger one on her nose. I must admit I was not expecting her request: she asked me to eradicate the wrinkles around her eyes.

Then there was the extremely obese woman who asked for a lip enlargement.

What is a surgeon to do in those cases? They have to lay their preconceptions aside and judge the case as presented. Would those ladies benefit from having the wrinkles removed or the lip enlargement? Can the desired outcome be achieved? Those are the operative questions, regardless of what else the surgeon thinks might be advisable.

There's something else to be said about this subject: the way you see yourself is different from the way other people see you.

In this context, I don't mean it in the psychological sense. I mean it in a more literal, physical sense. It's all about perspective and exactly where you're looking from. Let me explain:

A client once came to me and said "my thighs are different and uneven in shape." I simply couldn't see what she meant. I thought she was dealing in minutiae and I tried to convince her that it's normal, in fact it's almost inevitable, to have slight asymmetry between the left and right parts of the body.

But she was adamant and actually got quite indignant. "How can you not see that? You're supposed to be an expert!" she said. Finally I tried a different perspective: I stood right next to her, facing the same way, and looked over her shoulder and down the length of her body. From there I could see that, yes, one thigh did have slightly more bulge than the other.

This change in perspective makes a lot of difference, especially when a woman looks downwards at her hips and breasts; she will see them quite differently from how people see them when they look at her.

So, in a case like the one with that lady's thighs, should the difference be corrected by surgery or not? There are no hard and fast answers. It has to be a matter of common sense. If 10 people were shown the feature that the patient was presenting, and they could see it without being prompted, then it is a defect that is worth addressing.

But if eight of those 10 people would not be able to see a problem, that's something the patient should be advised to go away and think about carefully, before insisting on going ahead with surgery.

Fear is not necessarily a bad thing

The delight that the press has in exposing "botched jobs," plus the fact that many in my profession have been sued on completely frivolous, trumped-up charges of malpractice: these factors can induce a state of fear in even the most stoical surgeon.

I make a point of not letting it get to me. I haven't been sued in the course of my practice and I intend to keep it that way. I'm correctly qualified, I'm honest and transparent and I concern myself only with the patient's safety, maintaining the highest standards of professionalism and doing my utmost to satisfy my clients. I can't do more than that and, actually, I don't have to; by doing those simple things, I'm fulfilling all my obligations.

I remind myself that in a sense, all these law suits that fly around can serve to keep a good surgeon on their toes and motivate them to be excellent at all times.

Finally, I remind myself that F.E.A.R stands for False Emotions Appearing Real.

And if none of that works, I go home, wrap myself around my favourite pillow and scream.

The Arnie Syndrome

Throughout this book, I've promised to be honest. As part of that, I have to admit that I am occasionally faced with dilemmas; times when I've found it difficult to decide what to do, because there are such strong arguments on either side. Here's one of them:

Crazy demands in this industry are not in short supply. One of the craziest I've known came from a man who wanted to have a jaw implant, to make his jaw much more pronounced and stronger looking. He made no pretense of the fact that he wanted to look like Arnold Schwarzenegger; in fact that is exactly what he said.

This was a very young, athletically built man and he'd come to me six months earlier, saying he wanted a full facelift. I had refused, so he had gone to another country to have the facelift done. The result was devastatingly visible and he obviously was not satisfied.

So he came to me for help again, this time asking for some liposuction as well. Once again, I refused. Once again, he found someone else who did it for him, rather badly.

Now he was back for the third time, with this request to get a jaw like Schwarzenegger.

What to do?

It occurred to me this time that if I didn't do it, somebody else would, for sure. And it is a very delicate procedure that can develop terrible complications. I have a good record for cranio-facial procedures like these, and I knew I could do it well. So I used an implant to give him the look he was looking for.

A few days later he looked at it and said "I don't like it. Remove it." So I went back in and did as he requested.

This young man clearly suffered from dysmorphic body disease, which we talked about earlier. By conventional norms, he was a good looking man with no need for any surgical enhancement whatsoever; but in his own eyes he was a pitiful, ugly wretch. If he ever asks me to do anything for him again I will refuse and urge him to go and get the psychiatric help which is what he really needs.

When it turns into an addiction

I haven't seen any statistics on this, but it would be my educated guess that the vast majority of people who have plastic surgery only have it once, to correct something that has been stopping them from getting on with life the way they want to. Some may have it a few times, but not much more than three. But there are some people, sometimes celebrities, almost always very wealthy, who have it done multiple times. The result is rarely good. These people can be described as addicts.

Plastic surgery addiction is not a scientific nomenclature, but any experienced surgeon will have case notes on people who repeatedly ask for their help, either for the same body part or different parts.

At its most positive, it may happen because patients are so happy with the result they've achieved, they keep coming back to correct other areas because they now know the benefits it can bring. On the other hand it may be due to an obsession to correct a relatively minor defect that is not noticeable to others. Or it may be an obsessive desire to have similar features as close as possible to a famous person; possibly the same unhealthy impulse that turns people into celebrity stalkers.

Some people can become addicted to the anticipation, the excitement and the attention they receive. Successful procedures are often accompanied afterwards by a feeling of real euphoria when the patient sees how much better they look. That's fabulous and perfectly natural.

But it's also natural for the high to fade, for life to go back to normal and all the mundane, day-to-day problems to come back. At this point, some people are prompted to go back for another fix; after that amazing sense of wellbeing from one procedure, they think they might feel even better if they have another.

Well, maybe they will. It's not impossible. But seeking plastic surgery because of the buzz it might or might not bring is really not a wholesome motivation for doing it. And if the number of procedures carried out purely for aesthetic reasons starts creeping up, the warning light really should start to flash. The surgeon really needs to get down now and ask some searching questions about what the patient really wants.

If a patient comes to a surgeon and they already have a catalogue of past procedures, that is as clear a sign as is needed. But a good surgeon might also be able to spot someone who has unsound reasons for wanting a procedure and the potential to become an addict, even if they have never had any work done.

The warning signs are:

- Excessive preoccupation with physical appearance

- Strong belief that he or she has an abnormality or defect in appearance that makes them ugly

- Frequently examining themselves in the mirror or, conversely, avoiding mirrors altogether

- Believing that others take special notice of their appearance in a negative way

- Frequent cosmetic procedures with little satisfaction

- Excessive grooming, such as hair plucking

- Refusing to appear in pictures

- Skin picking

- Avoiding social situations

- Wearing excessive makeup or clothing to camouflage perceived flaws.

Denial is not a river in Egypt

While we're talking about the psychological aspects, we should mention denial. It's a syndrome that plastic surgeons encounter often, because we meet so many people who see themselves very differently to the way other people see them. Also, we meet people who are pinning all their hopes on plastic surgery, thinking that it is going to solve all their problems; and that's all too often a denial of reality.

Denial is a defense mechanism postulated by Sigmund Freud, in which a person is faced with a fact that is too uncomfortable to accept so they reject it instead, insisting that it is not true, even in the face of overwhelming evidence.

In some cases, a little denial is not necessarily a bad thing. In fact, a short period of it can be a healthy coping mechanism, giving people time to adjust to a painful or stressful event such as divorce or bereavement. It might also be a precursor to making some sort of fundamental change in a person's life. But being in denial for too long can prevent a person from effectively dealing with issues that require action, and especially from making wise, informed decisions.

So how do you overcome it? Ultimately, you can't; the only person who can overcome self-denial is the self who is doing the denying!

What you can do is suggest to the person that there may be another way of looking at the picture, then present the alternative view to them. You can be fairly sure they'll think about what you've said and, over time, may come round to seeing it the way you suggested.

But when you do it, make sure to keep your words calm, quiet and tactful. You're dealing with an extremely sensitive subject and if you make the person more defensive by being too blunt or aggressive, you're wasting your breath.

Managing expectations

My job is all about delicate operations. But the most delicate are the ones that happen in my consulting room, not in the theatre. The ones where I'm not using a scalpel to work with the patient's body, but using my words and intelligence to work with their psyche and ego.

Managing their expectations is a big part of that and it's always a tough call. It's somewhat complicated by the fact that expectations work both ways, for the surgeon and patient. My role can be described as restoring harmony to the patient. In effect. after working with us, they have to feel happy in their own skin. So I advise them upfront what can be done and what's possible. Identify to them which can be met and avoid giving them false hopes. Patients tend to have vivid imaginations, which is why, it's important to tell it as it is.

I'm gratified to say that it usually works for the best; most of the time clients are ecstatic. But nothing is guaranteed. I can't access their imagined outcome and neither can they mine. The difference is that they are the only ones that matter, not me. They are the ones that have to feel good about what we did together, to feel justified that they made the correct decision to entrust me with the surgery. And they have to live with it for the rest of their lives.

So I have to let their expectations and feelings overrule mine. If I'm not satisfied with the result but the patient is perfectly happy, I stifle my own inclination to proceed further. I try not to point out things that in my opinion need more work.

But what if I'm satisfied with the surgery but the client is not? I'm certainly not going to say "bad luck" to them, but neither am I going to step down from my belief that I did a good job. So we need to talk, in depth. We need to cover all these points and check them off:

- Was a realistic goal set?

- Was that goal met?

- Would a further session make a significant difference?

The problem is, as it is with anything that involves visual appreciation, it's terribly subjective. Some people like the colour purple and think it would look nice in their bedroom, others don't. Some people think a cute, button nose is much more attractive than a full Roman nose. Others don't.

At all times, I'm reminded by a quote from H. Jackson Brown Jr, one of the pioneers of my profession: "never deprive someone of hope, it might be all they have."

Handling people's fragile hopes is a huge responsibility, but it's something I just have to live with and deal with.

It's a man thing

From the sandy beaches of the Bahamas to the Gold Coast of Australia, from New York to LA, Chicago to Shanghai and Liverpool to Lima, from the ever rising number of gyms and aesthetic surgery clinics you see in every town, one thing is obvious; body consciousness is rocketing.

Perhaps the biggest surprise and certainly the biggest change is that it's no longer confined to women; men are every bit as dedicated in their quest for a perfect body and can often be even more vain than the ladies.

An increasing number of ordinary men are preoccupied with their appearance. They work their tails off to have a body like the ones they see on aftershave and underwear commercials, the images the media bombards them with all day, every day (and I'm sure more than a few women will smile wryly at this and think it's about time they had their turn.)

Up to a point, it's fine. It involves health, fitness, exercise and good dietary choices, which can never be a bad thing. The problem comes if and when they fail to create the body they dream of and become despondent.

Such mindsets can lead to crippling anxieties over self-esteem. For evidence, look no further than the growing number of eating disorders among males.

It all started in the 80s, or so it seems to me. That was when style suddenly became a Holy Grail and started being spelt with a capital S. Style. Now, decades later, fashion magazines and advertising agencies dictate the incredibly narrow, almost Fascistic, concept of what male beauty is all about.

Before then, men didn't define themselves as men in the same manner that women defined themselves as women; they didn't have the same highly developed self-consciousness about their being.

Imagine being a bright spark in a magazine publishing company and suggesting that, instead of magazines about fishing, cars, hi-fis or photography, men might actually buy and enjoy a title that was focused mainly around the idea of being a man, in the same way that women buy magazines about being a woman.

Just over a generation ago, the bosses would have laughed at you. Now they'd tell you to go away and think of something new.

What do I think of it? Professionally, I cannot possibly deny, it's good news for me. Personally, it worries me quite a lot. But history goes in cycles and nothing lasts forever. Who knows what the future will bring?

Heartbreaks of the trade

This job isn't always fun, not by any means.

My most challenging time was when I had to operate on my three month old nephew. My attachment to the child made the pressure very nearly unbearable, but it had to be done and it had to be done by me. It was like walking a tightrope, but thank goodness I was able to accomplish it, without any hitches.

I wish I could say the same about an episode I had with my own son. Out of his playful nature, he met an accident that left his face lacerated. With a plastic surgeon for a father, you would naturally expect Dad to step up and perform a flawless surgery, so they'd all live happily ever after. But the awful truth was, I wasn't around; I was away when it happened.

He still has quite a distinct scar to this day and every time I see it on him, I regret not being there. It's just too ironic.

Old smokey

On the other hand, this job can bring some unexpected happy bonuses.

I had a patient who had a very pinched nose. She had hardly ever breathed through her nose for most of her life; she was a classic mouth breather. This only came out in our consultation as she had originally asked for surgery on her nose purely to improve the appearance. But in doing that, I also made it functional and enabled her to breathe through it.

The next day, the first thing she said to me was, "you know what doctor? Smoking is bad. It smells horrible. I've been smoking all my life and never realised how bad it smells. And I promise I won't smoke ever again."

To end this miscellany of thoughts, here are some of my favourite quotes about surgery:

"It takes five years to learn when to operate and 20 years to learn when not to."

"Without love of people, a doctor cannot function effectively for long and can never establish the requisite interpersonal relationships with patients . . . . a genuine affection for patients is essential if one is to absorb ingratitude without anger, weariness without irritability, criticism without rancour."

"Surgery, like war, is hard. But it is better than war. It saves lives and binds men and women of good will together in deepest friendship."

"The surgeon must have a heart of a lion, the eyes of a hawk, and the hands of a woman."

And here's my favourite plastic surgery joke (warning: adults only!)

A woman visited a plastic surgeon who told her about a new procedure called 'The Knob,' where a small knob is placed at the top of the woman's head. The knob can then be turned to tighten up the skin and produce the effect of a brand new face-lift.

Of course, the woman wanted one. Over the course of the years, she kept tightening the knob and the effects were wonderful. The woman remained young looking and vibrant.

But after 15 years, she returned with two problems.

"All these years, everything has been working just fine," she said. "I've turned the knob many times and I've always loved the results. But now I've developed two annoying problems. First, I have these terrible bags under my eyes and the knob won't get rid of them."

"The doctor looked at her closely and said, "those aren't bags, those are your breasts."

She said, "well, I guess there's no point asking about the goatee."

Plastic Surgery as a Career

This chapter is aimed first and foremost at people who might be thinking of becoming a plastic surgeon. But if that doesn't describe you, please don't skip this yet.

It will bring you some interesting insights on what it takes to be fully qualified and how the business works, which is useful background if you want to develop an informed and balanced opinion of this profession.

The preliminaries

To say that getting educated in this discipline takes a long time is like saying it gets quite warm around the Equator. It takes over 11 years to be fully qualified and legitimately described as expert in plastic or aesthetic surgery.

Basic medical training, as your probably know, lasts five and a half years. Then another three years of post graduate studies are required to become a qualified surgeon. But this is a compulsory pre-requisite before you can focus exclusively on plastic surgery (or at least it should be compulsory; if you've read the earlier chapters, you'll know what my views are on under-qualified cosmetic surgeons!)

Once you do embark on plastic surgery as a sole discipline, you have another three years of training. During this period, you will be exposed to all the different aspects.

As well as aesthetic surgery, which is the best known form of plastic surgery and the one this book mostly deals with, there are a number of specialisations.

Hand surgery, for example, is a specialisation that corrects traumatic injuries or loss of function in the hand resulting from diseases like advanced arthritis.

Microvascular surgery specialises in connection and reconnection of tiny blood vessels, smaller 5 mm in diameter, restoring circulation before the affected part dies.

Craniofacial surgery addresses congenital and acquired deformities of the skull, face and jaws. This often involves manipulation of bone, skin, muscle and teeth, but does not extend to brain or eye procedures.

There are also surgeons who specialise in general reconstructive surgery for burns, or who focus on localised parts of the body such as the lower limbs and genitals.

You will get the opportunity to be exposed to many of these specialist areas during your dedicated training period, so you'll have every chance to evaluate and see which one is your calling.

Gore galore

It may be something that goes without saying, but I've even known doctors from other branches of medicine who aren't keen on the sight of too much blood and guts. So let's just emphasise that this profession is not for the faint of heart. In the course of it, you will inevitably be exposed to the goriest and most unsightly images you'll see for as long as you live, not to mention a range of smells that are simply indescribable.

I remember once, when I hadn't been working in ER as a junior resident for more than a few days, a young lad came in with an iron rod stuck in his neck as if it was a javelin. It had penetrated just inches away from his spine, which would have paralysed him for life. I have to admit I almost lost it. But I managed to hold it together and the team who did the procedure were competent enough to remove the rod successfully.

Naturally, you get used to it over time and reach a point where you don't think twice about it. Recently, I was working with one of our senior nurses and a young intern, removing liters of stinking, putrid matter from inside a patient's body. It was a long, tiring job, so when the senior nurse suggested stopping for lunch and finishing the job afterwards, I was happy to agree.

While the senior nurse and I were wolfing down a plate of spaghetti bolognese, I caught sight of the young intern staring at us in horror, as if we were a pair of ghouls. She herself had chosen a green salad and was having trouble touching it.

She got past her squeamishness in the end. You have to.

Make a commitment and more

Once you decide plastic surgery is the career of your choice, you have to be totally committed to it, passionate and willing to give everything you've got to accomplish your objectives.

This isn't just a string of platitudes. Let me say again, your dedication has to be exceptional. This is something that requires energy, enthusiasm, day-long concentration, attention to detail, focus and, perhaps above all, a vast reservoir of patience.

You will also need flexibility and a mind that's open to the constant updates and innovations that will come your way. Being aware of industry advances through constantly reading and attending conferences conducted by peers and colleagues is as much a part of the job as any other aspect.

Once you have amassed enough experience, it's also part of your duty as a medical practitioner to share what you know. As well as helping other professionals, this actually sharpens and broadens your own mind and opens you to new ways of seeing things. It reminds me of the old saying, "iron sharpens iron."

Money isn't everything

It's undeniable that being a plastic surgeon is well paid. With the amount of training and the dedication and responsibility involved, I think it is appropriate.

But as with any noble profession, it is unwise to solely consider the financial gain in your decision to follow it. You must set aside

---

the notion of personal rewards and devote yourself to fulfilling the oath you have professionally sworn to uphold.

And as you progress through your career and come into contact with peers, please don't use money as a yardstick for their worth and achievement. It should never be the be all and end of all of any surgeon's career.

My cricket captain once told me, "go on the pitch, play your game correctly and the runs will automatically come." This is the same basic principle I have applied professionally: work properly and the money will follow you.

Get yourself mentored

During the early part of my career, I had the privilege to work under the tutelage of a highly successful and popular plastic surgeon, whom I considered my mentor. I observed him working on children and trauma patients with deformities, from nine in the morning to five in the afternoon, non-stop. He applied himself to every operation from the first to the last of the day with the same amazing enthusiasm, energy and expertise.

Then, straight after five I used to see him disappear, with several of the other assistant doctors, nurses and staff on his team. At weekends I did not see any of them except for hospital staff and some of the doctors if there was an emergency. This was unusual and it made me curious and, yes, a bit envious of them. So one day I asked him a question which actually had a hidden agenda; I was hoping it might lead me to find out whatever it was they all did once they'd left the hospital.

I asked him, "is it OK if I use the facility to do some reading and research after five and on weekends? I get a bit bored with nothing to do."

He said, "don't you want to enjoy your life?"

I said, "yes, of course, but for me to do that, I have to learn well."

The answer must have pleased him because he said "come over to the centre after six."

And that's how I found out. It turned out that they left so promptly at five because that was the start of their one hour rest period. At six, he and his team of assistants and nurses started doing aesthetic procedures and they had a long list of patients.

After this he became my mentor, and the amount of guidance he has given me along the way simply cannot be calculated or repaid. If you're learning plastic surgery, I urge you to try and find a mentor too, although you can be a bit more straightforward about it than I was!

If there's a senior colleague whose work you admire and you feel they would make a good mentor, just tell them you would like to learn from them however, whenever and wherever it is practical and—of course—offer to assist their work in any way you can. They can only say no and, more often than not, they'll say OK.

Perseverance furthers

Just the other night, in a rare bit of leisure time I had to myself, I watched a documentary on the Discovery Channel. It featured a leopard with a heavy prey, trying to drag it up a tree so it could be eaten without intrusion from other predators.

The lifeless prey was heavy and it kept slipping from the leopard's grip. On and on it went, over and over again, time after time. Leopard climbs with heavy prey, prey falls, leopard climbs back down.

Finally the leopard gathered enough strength, grabbed the prey one more time, started climbing and this time reached the top of tree.

I was so inspired by that. The lesson it has for aspirant plastic surgeons is clear. There is a vast amount to learn, it takes years, there are endless challenges in your training and there will be times when you will feel discouraged. But never give up, keep pushing forward to your goal.

I know there's a saying that somewhat contradicts my tale of the persistent leopard, which is that "insanity is doing the same thing over and over again without success, but with the expectation that somehow the outcome will be different."

There's a difference though, because if you keep plugging away at this as a chosen profession, a truly wonderful outcome awaits.

Fast forward to . . . organising a practice

OK, you've got your qualification, you've clocked up the necessary experience and the time has come to set up a practice of your own. Let's look at that in some detail, because it requires a great deal of thought.

What they don't tell you at school

When you're learning to be a plastic surgeon, they teach you all about medicine, they teach you all about diseases, they teach you how problems are presented and the best possible treatment for them.

They don't tell you much about how to be a successful doctor to begin with.

How to approach on the patient's psyche, how to get the best out of the people who will report to you, how to look after the logistics behind a successful operation, how to keep yourself constantly motivated—year in, year out—are all skills you must acquire.

You pick up a lot of them along the way. But that learning process takes a quantum leap when you set up your own practice.

It's one hell of a ride!

So what does it take to succeed?

When you reach this point in your career, you will find that—like it or not—just being a doctor doesn't cut it anymore. You have to wear several hats to make your practice exceptional and truly worth your and your patients' while. Here are the components that you'll need:

Component one: a surgeon

To stand out, a plastic surgeon nowadays not only needs to be a good doctor, he needs to be a great one; well rounded, informed and fully equipped to perform his chosen craft. From an ethical standpoint, he has to be impeccable and precise in everything he does, since this is the prime reason why patients will want to come come and seek his professional advice.

Component two: an artist

He has to be able to see the big picture even in the smallest procedure. he has to have a vision of how his work will harmonise with the rest of the patient's body.

Component three: a diplomat

He has to be able to engage, converse and reassure people from all kinds of background and in all kinds of state of mind. He needs flexibility, discernment, intuition and insight in his interaction with people so he can quickly get an accurate feel for them and what they really want. And he has to satisfy them that he is always at their service, willing and able to help.

Component four: an administrator

Managing a practice requires outstanding administrative skills. The necessary attention to detail is quite immense. It's not the first thing you think of when you consider a career in plastic surgery; in fact it might never even cross your mind that you will need this skill. But believe me, you will.

Component five: a businessman

Without being blinded to his primary raison d'etre, he needs to ensure the viability of his practice at all times. This means being conscious on a daily basis of the practice's financial position and able to take decisive action if any aspect of it needs scrutiny, adjustment or correction.

Once you know how, the next question is where

There's a saying that seems to have slipped into common usage these days: "location, location, location." It's attributed to a man called William Dillard, who ran a very successful chain of department stores in the US. He said it in response to someone who asked him to state the three main ingredients of a successful store.

It applies to more or less any place where people come to buy goods and services, whatever they are, and our profession is no exception.

You have to determine first the area where you plan to serve. There has to be a high number of potential users of what you offer within the immediate area; setting up shop in a beautiful but remote place in the country might give you nice views but it won't help your business.

Your prospective patients need to be able to find you and get to you easily. Which usually means the centre has to be in a well known urban thoroughfare, easily reached by both private and public transport. As an alternative, you could choose a residential area, as long as it's respectable and well looked after; preferably with other medical practices already in the neighbourhood. Side streets and back alleys are an obvious no-no!

Wherever it is, parking space is a must as your patients' comfort has to be foremost.

When patients walk in, they must find themselves in a place that encourages their confidence. Professional, welcoming, discreet and of course spotlessly clean and tidy are the watchwords here. There must be facilities for aesthetic and plastic surgery patients can be separately taken care of without interfering with each other.

I started my practice in a small space and an inconspicuous location, but I was able to draw patients there because I had established a good "word of mouth" reputation. But I realised it was tedious for my clients to get there and I moved as soon as I was able to.

When you think about these matters, it's very useful to try and see it from the customer's viewpoint, not yours. The customer is king and they deserve to be treated that way.

Obviously, providing quality, comfort and convenience will have an impact on the cost of your service. But as you may know by now, I don't believe that this business has any room at all for cost cutting.

Having said all that, I am aware that in my native India there are many dedicated plastic surgeons who don't have any premises at all. These amazing guys travel miles to serve their patients and they work wherever they can. I truly take my hat off to these fantastic people.

A question of charges

Like all my colleagues, I have to perform a balancing act between treating people who can afford to pay for it and those who may need it even more, but don't have the money.

I believe it's important to serve both. The trick lies, as I say, in finding the balance. Too much of one kind and you end up out of pocket, which isn't fair. Too much of the other and you're failing in your moral and human duty. And naturally, you have to provide the same high level of service to everyone you treat.

It's not all that easy but it is vital that you keep this one in perspective.

Training is what keeps it turning

Teamwork defines the practice you lead. So it's important to have on board like minded teammates who are self motivated and able to really contribute through their actions.

The training and guidance you provide them are essential in ensuring you get the best from them and help them to be better individuals, so they can handle all many different pressures their job throws at them.

In this modern era of specialisation, I quite often come across people who are looking for staff positions in my practice but are limited in the particular job they are able—or willing—to do.

This is only my opinion and other practitioners might not agree, but I believe that people at staff level need to be able to

---

multi-task, at least to some extent. But I do accept that if they're willing to learn additional skills, I have to be willing to provide the training that will help them to master them.

In particular, I go out of my way to train them in the commercial aspect of the practice and instill an entrepreneurial spirit in them. It gives me enormous satisfaction to see people from my team go out on their own and become entrepreneurs themselves.

It's a policy that has paid off for us. When people have a better broad understanding of what it takes to run a successful group or an enterprise, and what other people are doing to play their part in it, everyone gets along better and performs that way too.

Expanding the practice

When the time comes to expand, it's also time to think about partnership.

I know this isn't a prospect that all surgeons relish, as they like to be sole controllers of their own destiny. But the fact is, if you're successful, you will eventually reach a point where you don't have enough hours in the day or pairs of hands to cope with the demand.

This is when you need to reach out and combine with other surgeons to form a team.

My advice would be to look for people with skill sets that complement yours. This means that clients can enjoy more of a

---

one-stop service, where the facilities they need are integrated conveniently.

As I've said before, you don't want to come across like a supermarket, as it can have a diluting or cheapening effect on what we do. But on the other hand, it's good to be able to broaden your range of services so they at least cover the areas that are most in demand.

Room at the top

There is a lot of room at the top of the profession, but its a long hard climb, and there is no elevator running above the lower floors; you have to make the ascent under your own steam.

Some people wait in life for an elevator to start, or take a lift that only goes part of the way. Others sit down and bitch about the strivers who toiled up the stairs. "Many things come to he who waits, but seldom the things he waits for."

What does it all mean?

At this stage of my practice and my life, I think success is simply a matter of making my patients, my staff and my family, happy. I have embraced the fact that serving others' interests above mine is a destiny well worth striving for.

The gratification I get when patients and clients recognise my efforts is an immense feeling, which to me is success of the highest order.

Want to achieve it too? In any given opportunity, treat your patient and staff as you would treat your family. Be ethical, technical and professional, compassionate, concerned and caring in addressing both your patients' and your staff's needs.

Above all, just be honest and half the battle is won. Be caring and the war is over.

Conscience at Work: The Surgeon's Social Responsibility

The medical profession as a whole takes the position that good health is a right, not a privilege. We in the plastic surgery profession feel the same way; a normal appearance and function can be claimed as a right as well.

This is why we try to help people who cannot afford our normal fees but who are being held back in life because of an unsightly but correctable aspect of their appearance.

For instance, I helped an elderly man who lost his job and could not be taken seriously as a candidate for another one, because he had an abnormal plump fold of flesh that hung down from under his chin. I also helped a penniless young actress with a straightforward procedure to alter her large nose and small chin.

Yes, these were purely cosmetic procedures but they made a vast difference to the number of job offers they both received, so their effect was socially valid and practically useful.

Then there are the countless numbers of children with cleft palettes, burn victims and people suffering post-trauma

---

deformities. Reconstructive surgery is often needed by people who come from the lower rungs of society. They don't have the money or insurance cover to pay for it themselves and the state does not have the budget or facilities to provide it.

In many cases, these patients receive operations which are funded by the plastic surgeons themselves; it's a common practice all over the world.

Where does the money come from?

It's no secret in our industry that the money a surgeon makes from cosmetic surgery is what finances the re-constructions they perform. Every surgeon will tell you that.

Taking from the rich to help the poor is, of course, not a new idea. George Jacob, a good friend and colleague of mine, came up with the phrase "Robin Hood surgery" and it appeals to me a lot. But please don't take it out of context— we don't rob our rich patients, we just re-distribute some of their wealth!

From every point of view, I think someone who is well established in my profession must see it as a moral responsibility to contribute to the Robin Hood movement. I work in India, where I'm from, and Dubai where I live, on a charitable, pro bono basis. In India, we provide free surgeries, sponsor a scholarship fund for deserving students and support organisations which care for orphans. In Dubai we work closely with one particular foundation to treat patients who from Iraq and Afghanistan with traumas and injuries.

But without a lucrative practice, I could not even think about engaging in benevolent activities.

CSR—or Corporate Social Responsibility—is a bit of a buzzword nowadays and many multinational conglomerates make at least a token attempt to implement a CSR program. I think doctors should have such a program formally implemented within their practice. It will make the world a better place to live in if we all contribute to making it one.

As part of my contribution to that better world, all the proceeds from this book will be used to finance surgery for children who require it. I take this opportunity to offer heartfelt thanks to you and to all my patients who, consciously or not, have helped me in that effort.

Finally, A Few Testimonials

B.A., a 29 year-old lawyer who had breast augmentation:
There is so much I can say enough about Dr.Sanjay and his able staff. I was made to feel I was taken care of at every step of the process. The nurses and anesthetist were amazing on the day of surgery and set me worry free. I am so pleased with my experience and would recommend him to anyone interested in plastic surgery. Please note I had constricted breasts, which are difficult to "reverse", and I am happy to declare that I now look natural and symmetric.

K.L., a 42 year-old teacher who had eyelid surgery (blepharoplasty):
I have yet to come up with words to explain how happy I am with everything Dr. Sanjay has done. Being treated like any individual, he listened to me intently and explained to me the process I was having done. The time I wait to see the doctor was not that much, and when it is my turn he would give me his undivided attention. Simply he cares so much and it reflects towards me. He is amazing! I can't believe that someone as accomplished as he is, is also such a sincere person!

M.S., a 38 year-old homemaker who had a liposuction and tummy tuck
Appreciate the positive experience! Never felt for once I was a statistic. Level of professionalism is outstanding across all those involved, yet loving and caring. A rarity in today's medical

environment! I felt as though my heart was as well cared for as my body! Those of us who live in Dubai are truly fortunate to have such a fantastic surgeon.

A.S., a 53 year-old beauty consultant who had breast augmentation:

I've told everyone about the wonderful, professional and positive experience of being a patient of Dr. Parashar. He truly is a natural in helping people look and feel better. It has been my pleasure being cared for by such great people!!

M.R., a 39 year-old account manager who had pectoral implants:

Great job, Dr. Parashar! I was truly impressed with your skill as a surgeon and your sensitivity as a human being. You answered all my questions and did everything well on the surgery. Compliments to the office staff as well.

J.S., a 33 year-old physician and mother who had breast augmentation and lift:

I have already given word around about you and your staff to quite a few others (including my own patients!) You just know how to make a patient feel comfortable at all times, with your warmth and cozy work environment. You could sense everybody's excellence in what they had to do. The results are just great! Thank you is not enough for all the things you did for me.

G.B., a 59 year-old retired pharmacist who had a facelift, eye brow lift and eyelid surgery:

Never can forget the day of surgery, when all present were so genuinely concerned. Totally satisfied with the results. Recommendations have been made to all those who belong to my sphere of influence. I know Dr. Parashar will also do the same great job he did on me, because this is the standard of his practice. Excellent!

Like those who were about to undergo the procedure, there was uncertainty on my part post surgery. Then I got a call from Dr. Sanjay like a few hours later and it was comforting to know, I was going to be alright. Unbelievable! He truly takes time out to call his patients after the surgery.

G.A., a 40 year-old gym instructor who had fat transfer for lip enhancement:
I have nothing but praise for Dr. Parashar and his wonderful staff! Everyone in the office is awesome, and he truly cares and that means so much to each patient. I've referred everyone to your clinic. If I should ever consider any other type of plastic surgery, I know exactly where to go. Thanks!

E.B., a 22 year-old college student who had breast augmentation:
Y'all did a great! I love my new bosoms! I'm comparing them to other women's before and after photos and I could say mine are better! Dr. Parashar, great job sir and thanks! I'll see you soon for my follow-up appointment.

D.F., a 31 year-old stage actress who had cheek implants:
Thanks you Dr. Parashar and to everyone concerned. Your kindness and caring attitude made this a wonderful experience. I am very happy with my new look. Thanks again.

J.K., a 39 year-old mother who had a tummy tuck and liposuction:
Dr. Parashar is such an excellent doctor! He changed me inside out! Not only I improved my figure but also made me confident

---

that he was my right choice! Thanks Dr. Parashar, I love my new figure!

K.R., a 43 year-old financial advisor who had rhinoplasty:
From my initial phone call to the day of my surgery, the entire staff was very helpful, pleasant, knowledgeable and professional. Everyone was extremely helpful and informative! This is the total plastic surgery experience. I couldn't have asked for any more than I got during this emotional experience. I absolutely LOVE the results! I would refer others to Dr. Sanjay and his staff.

V.B., a 66 year-old who had a facelift, eyelid surgery, and chin implant:
Much to love about my experience with Dr. Parashar. Everyone was so friendly from day one and making me feel right at home. Should there be any future surgeries that I have will be done, it'll be by him of course. Results are fabulous as was every bit of my experience.

P.L., a 51 year-old high school principal who had an arm lift (brachioplasty):
Treatment both before and after surgery was a delightful experience. Had all the reference material about before surgery (on what to expect, what to do, what not to do, and how to speed my recovery) and covered any question I may have had. Totally worry free!

A.D., a 35 year-old fashion designer who had a tummy tuck, body lift, and breast lift after losing over 140 pounds:
I've never been to a doctor's office where every member of the staff were more than nice, polite, and helpful as everyone I met in your office. I felt very comfortable from my first visit on.

I've recommended Dr. Parashar to several people already and I'm pretty sure they will come as well. So happy with my results and sing your praises regularly! Thank you so very much!

N.A., a 40 year-old oral surgeon who had breast augmentation:
I am completely thrilled with my entire experience. From phone calls to consultation to surgery and follow-up, I found everyone at Dr. Sanjay's clinic to be helpful, informative, professional, and enjoyable! I would not hesitate to recommend friends to you! Thanks to all of you for a great experience!

S.F., a 61 year-old freelance editor and part time musician who had a facelift and eyelid tuck:
Dr. Parashar and his staff treated me like an old friend! They are all simply wonderful! Rock on!

K.C., a 28 year-old dry-wall hanger who had rhinoplasty:
Everyone I met that worked with Dr. ParashaR and himself made me feel so comfortable in all ways. I never had to wait. I was always called right in. Dr. Sanjay made you feel like you were his only concern at the time he was talking to you. I would gladly recommend him to anyone.

M.R., a 46 year-old physical therapist who had breast augmentation and breast lift:
So pleased with my breast augmentation. All of my appointments (consultation, pre-op and post op) went better than I expected and the surgery really surprised me, there were no problems at all and recovery was a breeze—even though Dr. Parashar kept telling me that not everyone recovers so fast. Everything went wonderful. Thank you all.

A.A., a 41 year-old who had a chin implant and neck liposuction:

I was very impressed and satisfied with my procedure and how well I was treated. The entire staff always has a smile on their face and a kind word. Dr. Parashar has a demeanour that evokes confidence and appreciation in his abilities. I'd recommend him to anyone who is interested without a doubt.

I.K., a 33 year-old flight attendant who had breast augmentation:

One of the best experiences of my life. I can't thank you enough.

V.T., a 26 year-old software developer who had liposuction:

Dr. Parashar, thank you for being so considerate and helping me through all the appointments and "fun stuff" I went through both before and after the surgery. Dr. Sanjay, I am so thrilled with my results and I am so much happier now that it is truly amazing. I am eternally grateful to you.

You have worked a miracle and I am glad that you helped me to achieve what I have always dreamed of having. wonderful thinner thighs. I can't thank you enough, and I will always keep you in mind if I or anyone else I should know could use your services. I couldn't have asked for or wished for a better Doctor.

You were there for me to ask questions before and after and you calmed my nerves on the day of the surgery. You were even there for me on a Saturday morning when I was sick. I don't know too many doctors that would care that much about their patients.

Your manner and how excited you were for me on what I looked like just a week after kept me going. I couldn't believe how excited you were for me—Again . . . I can't thank you enough. Thank you for being so considerate and nice. THANKS!!!

C.M., a 49 year-old sales manager who had an abdominoplasty (tummy tuck):
I would send any interested friend or family member to you. Everyone in the office is very friendly and I knew this right off the bat. During my first visit to gather info, that I would be having my surgery there! As for waiting to be seen, I don't think I've ever taken a seat in the waiting room; I've always been ushered in quickly to see the doctor. Dr. Parashar you did a wonderful job on my tummy. Thank you so much.